COLOUR

FOOD LOG

WATER LOG →

MONTHLY STATS

→

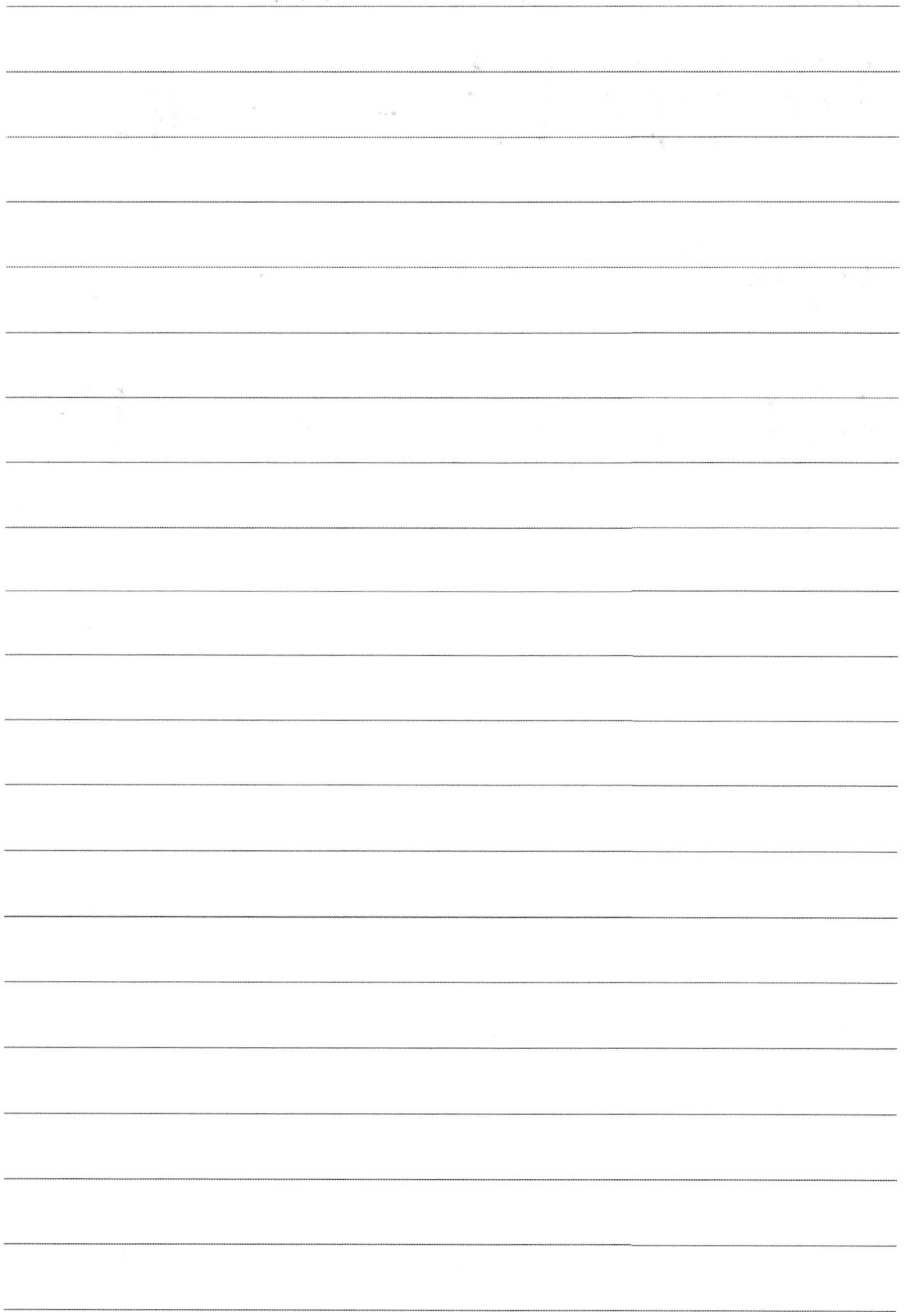

FOOD LOG : 10/02/19

Breakfast:

- hot cross bun
- croissant
- orange

Snack:

- banana
- thornton's chocolate
- chicken bite

Dinner:

- Chicken casserole

Snack:

- Duplo

2-3 cups
of water

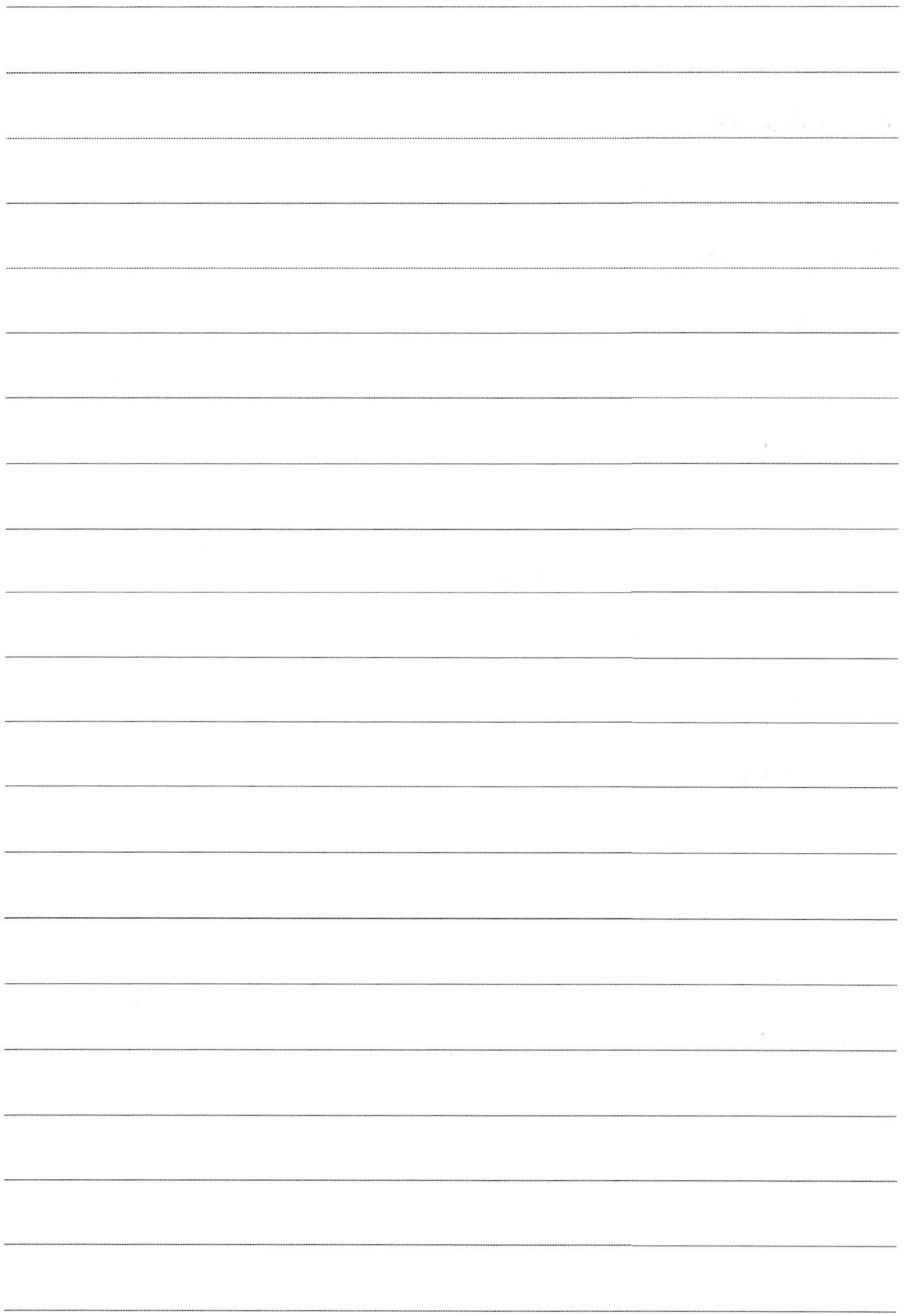

food log: 11/02/19

Breakfast:
- bowl of granola

Lunch:
- soup
- belvita soft bake

Snack:
- apple
- sweet potatoes (1)

4-5 cups
of water

Dinner:
- quiche
- bread

Snack:
- some Picaballa
- orange
- a slice of ham

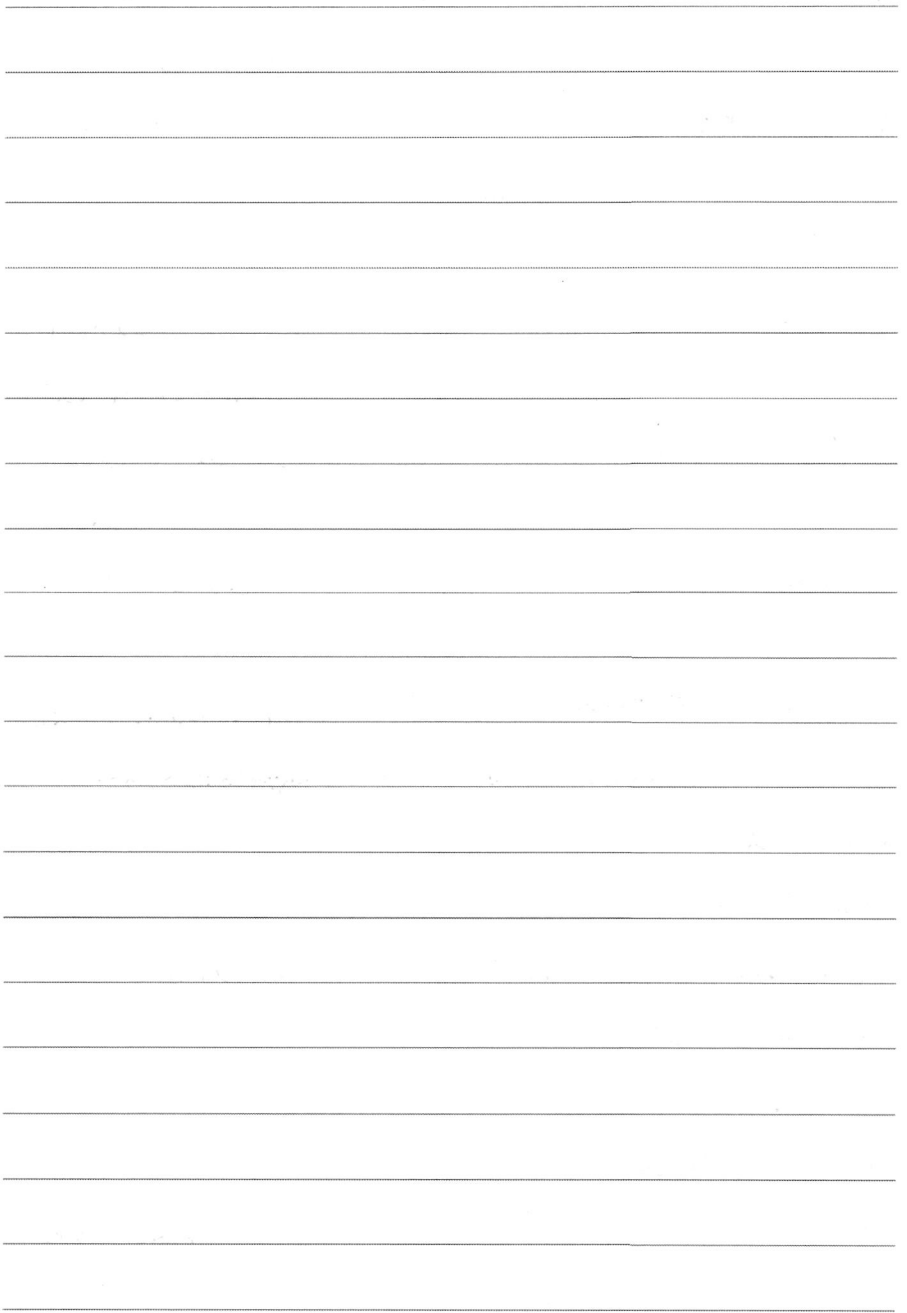

Amicinati a Sir Andrew+. Not to be abed after midnight, is to be up betimes, and diluculo surgere, thou know'st —

(Sir Andrew)

A false conclusion! I hate it as an unfilled can. To be up after midnight, and to go to bed then, is early; so that to go to bed after midnight is to go to bed betimes. Does not our life consist of the 4 elements?.

(Sir Andrew)

Th'art a scholar; let us therefore eat and drink. Marian, I say!. A stoup of wine!.

(Sir Andrew)

(Feste)

Welcome, ass. Now let's have a catch.

(Sir Andrew)

(Feste)

(Sir Andrew)

Come on, there is sixpence for you. Let's have a song.

(Sir Andrew)

(Feste)

A love song, a love song!.

(Sir Andrew)

(Feste)

(Sir Andrew)

bene, bene

(Feste)

(Sir Andrew)

A contagious breath.

(Sir Andrew).

To hear by the nose, it is dulcet in contagion. But shall we make the welkin dance indeed? Shall we rouse the night-owl in a catch that will draw thee souls out of one weaver? Shall we do that?

(Sir Andrew)

(Feste)

(Sir Andrew)

(Feste)

(Sir Andrew)

(Feste)

(Sir Andrew)

REVIOS

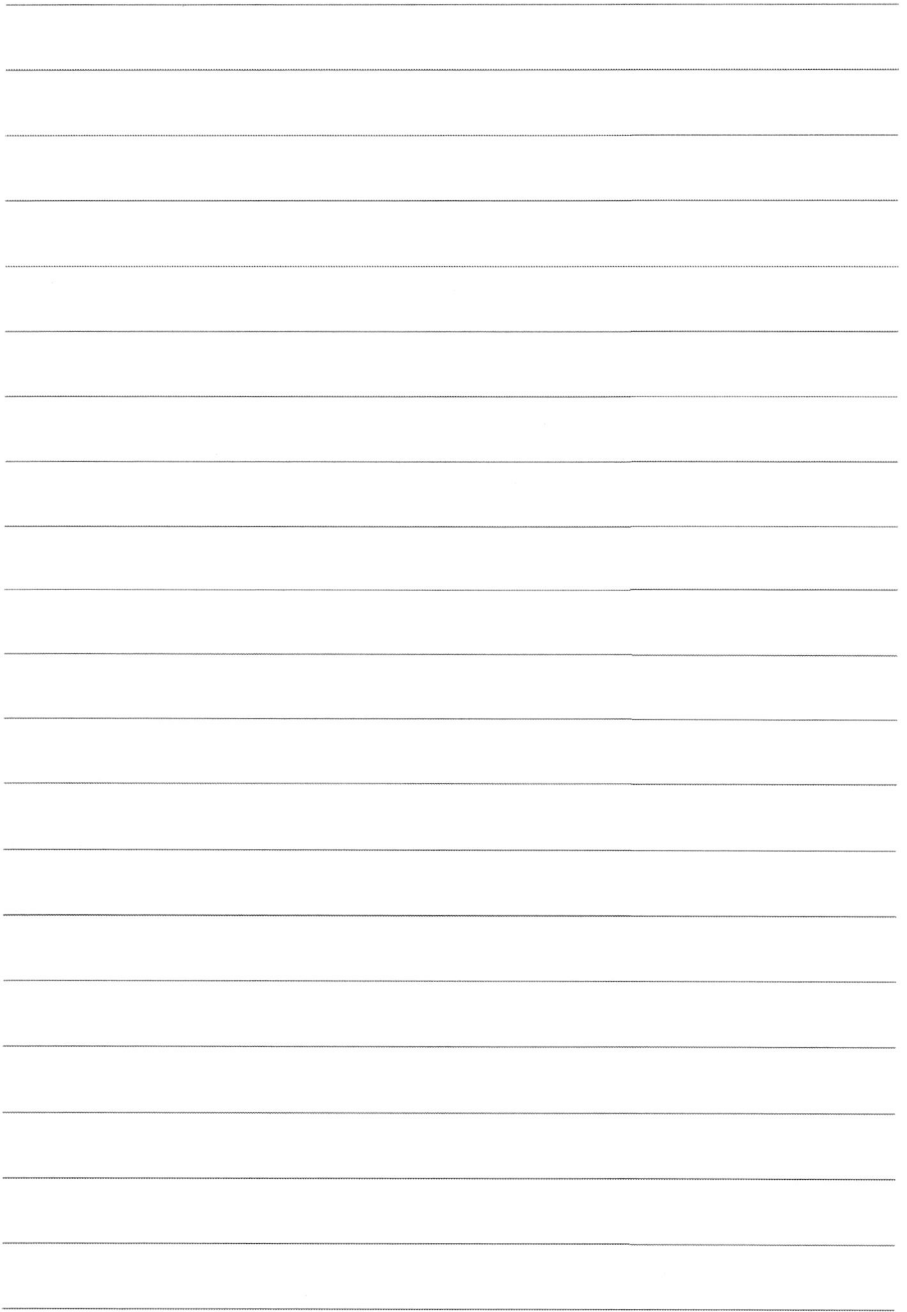

REVISION DIET: 2019

Breakfast :
- granola & yoghurt & banana
- egg
- 2 cups of water

Lunch :
- lunchbox

Dinner :
- smaller portions of carbs
- more salad

Snacks :
- fruit

NOTES:
- less carbs, more fruit & veg
- more water
- snack less, but snacks should be more fruit

Printed in Great Britain
by Amazon